The Invisible Alchemy

What's that smell? Oh, burnt toast,
A breakfast dish we love the most.
Add a pinch of laughter, a dash of cheer,
Our morning ritual is oh-so-clear.

Mixing stories with a twist of lime,
We toast to nights and silly rhyme.
Invisible magic we create,
In every moment, never too late.

Ripple Effects of Bonds

When one friend trips, we all fall down,
Rolling in laughter, no one's a clown.
The ripples spread in a joyful way,
Waving worries of the day away.

A prank that backfires, oh what a sight,
We cry with giggles, all through the night.
Each stone thrown creates a wave,
In the pond of joy, we misbehave.

Secrets Woven in Silence

In the corner, whispers creep,
A squirrel's stash, the secrets keep.
Underneath the garden gnome,
Lies a treasure, never roamed.

A cat's meow, a dog's soft bark,
In the yard, they make a mark.
A dance of shadows, laughter bounces,
While the neighbor's laundry flounders.

The Harmony of Interwoven Lives

Two socks lost in the laundry whirl,
The tale unfolds, a missing pearl.
A spatula and a fork in strife,
Yet they blend in a feast of life.

The fridge hums a silly song,
While a pickle dreams of where it belongs.
A dance of spices, a dash of fun,
In the kitchen where chaos is spun.

Ties Beyond the Surface

A rubber band that stretched too wide,
With gummy bears that take a ride.
A paperclip's ambition, soaring high,
Yet it's tangled in a secret lie.

The clock ticks loud, a ticklish tease,
While the cat sprawls, it aims to please.
Under the stairs, dust bunnies plot,
In a world where time is hot.

Heartstrings and Wavelengths

A tune from the radio, all out of whack,
As grandma dances with an old knickknack.
The toaster pops like a cheerful friend,
With edible gifts that never end.

A cookie jar whispers, 'Take a bite,'
While shadows waltz in the evening light.
In the chaos of crumbs and cheerful squeaks,
Lies a story that forever speaks.

Journeys Bound by Thread

A sock went missing, oh what a deal,
A journey began with a strange squeal.
The cat took off with a yarn ball,
While the dog chased a shadow, like a sudden call.

Through the tangled web of a playful chase,
A sweater unraveled, leaving just space.
They scurried around till the day turned night,
With a laugh and a sigh, oh what a sight!

Intertwined Echoes

Once a pair of shoes lost their mate,
To tango with slippers, what a fate!
They tapped on the floor, in a silly dance,
Owning the party with glee and chance.

An echo laughed back, from the wall it came,
Who knew such footwear could play such a game?
They pranced on the shelves, under the light,
In a world where footsteps could take flight!

Legends of the Boundless

A spoon and a fork had a grand debate,
Who was more important on a dinner plate?
The kettle chimed in, made a ruckus too,
While the plates just sighed, feeling quite blue.

Then came the napkins, folding with grace,
Chiming in rhythms, it got quite the pace.
They laughed and they quarreled, in the kitchen's glow,
In this culinary tale, chaos, don't you know?

The Fabric of Fate

In a quilt full of patches, stories were spun,
Each stitch a riddle, oh what fun!
With a cat on the corner, pawing the seam,
And a dog tugging gently on a wild dream.

Beneath the soft layers, mischief brewed bold,
As blankets conspired, their tales need be told.
With whispers and giggles, they spun all night,
In a fabric of laughter, the stars shone bright!

The Looming Dance of Stories

Once a penguin wore a tie,
He slid and slipped, oh my!
A fish laughed from the sea,
'You'll never catch me, wait and see!'

A cat joined in with a hat,
Pretending to chase after that.
But instead, she fell in mud,
Creating quite the messy thud!

The crowd gathered, all aglow,
With snacks and laughter in tow.
Each tale woven in the crowd,
Made the silly scenes so loud!

As stories tangled in the air,
A squirrel danced without a care.
With each twist and turn, they'd prance,
Enjoying every goofy chance.

Intersecting Paths of Fate

A frog in boots, so proud and bold,
Hopped on paths of stories told.
He met a hare with a broken shoe,
Together they conjured quite a view!

They rolled down hills, what a sight!
Chasing sunshine, laughing bright.
The moon peeked in, gave a wink,
'You silly pair, you seem to sync!'

A mouse with cheese tried to join,
But slipped and fell, oh the groin!
The frog just croaked with glee,
While the hare grinned, 'It's just a spree!'

As footsteps marched in twisty trails,
They shared their dreams, and told their tales.
In every chuckle and cheesy joke,
Life's wild dance was no mere hoax.

The Quilt of Shared Journeys

Patchwork stories, bright and bold,
A grandma's quilt is never old.
Each square a laugh or silly fight,
Stitched with love, laughter, delight.

A raccoon dropped a snack or two,
While dancing 'round in a tutu.
The squirrel giggled with each fall,
'Can I join in? I want to sprawl!'

The sky turned pink with playful glee,
As stories swirled, wild and free.
From fluffed-up pillows to silly dreams,
Life burst forth in snickers and gleams.

So here's to quilts and tales divine,
In every patch, a twist, a rhyme.
With laughter stitched right through the seams,
We cherish this in all our dreams!

Stories from the Fabric of Life

In a town where socks often roam,
A shoe thought it could find a home.
It tripped on a lace, fell on its face,
Now it waddles with quite a grace.

An old hat claims it has seen it all,
While a scarf wrapped up in a friendly brawl.
They laugh about days in the dusty attic,
Where they spun wild stories, oh so dramatic.

The mittens played charades with the gloves,
Making up tales of heroic doves.
Their yarns all tangled, but spirits stay bright,
In the wardrobe's laughter, from day to night.

So gather 'round and hear the cheer,
For life's little quirks bring endless dear.
Each stitch and seam tells a tale anew,
A patchwork of giggles, just waiting for you.

The Weaving of Dreams

In a world where pillows often scheme,
They plot and plan to host a dream.
A comforter joins, and they all align,
Whispering secrets over cups of brine.

Blankets are bullies, with wooly might,
Tickling toes in the dead of night.
While the curtains gossip, in swoops of flair,
Pulling in dust bunnies to join their affair.

The teddy bears roll in with a joke,
As a nightlight blinks, and the shadows poke.
Each soft toy chuckles, their laughter so deep,
Stirring the dreams that tumble from sleep.

And with morning's light, those tales will blend,
As shadows retreat, but giggles extend.
In pillows and blankets, behold what we glean,
A tapestry woven with hiccups unseen.

Kinships Crafted in Silence

Two plates sat quietly on the shelf,
Whispering stories of dinner's wealth.
With forks sharing secrets, and spoons getting bold,
Each meal a canvas, a joy to behold.

A ladle chimes in with a hearty laugh,
Recalling the times of the kitchen's half.
While spices together dance in twirls,
Mixing up memories, like old silly swirls.

The table, a witness to all that unfolds,
Collects every tale, in shards and in folds.
With tablecloth wrinkles, like laughter lines,
Echoing dinners where friendship shines.

So gather your forks and raise your cups high,
For kinships grow close, under the same sky.
In every bite, there's a tale to tease,
Food binds us together, with laughter and ease.

Echoes of Interconnection

A pair of boots, with stories to share,
Chasing shadows on the way to nowhere.
While umbrellas argue on who should stay,
Fighting the breeze, come what may.

A bicycle chimes with a spinning tale,
Of adventures taken along the trail.
Wheels turning stories of sun and of rain,
In a dance of freedom, joy, and some strain.

The sunshine beams with a cheeky grin,
As it beams down on the mishaps within.
Every tumble and trip, a laugh to extend,
Within this adventure, the joy will not end.

So take a step back, and see how we fit,
In this quirky world, we all can commit.
Each moment a stitch in the fabric of fun,
An ever-woven journey for everyone.

The Hand that Stitches

In a world of thread and needle,
Where laughter hides in seams,
A hand that stitches stories bright,
Frolics between the dreams.

One loop is for the silly pranks,
A knot for every quirk,
With yarn that tells of dancing cats,
And socks that go to work.

It juggles buttons like a clown,
And paints with every hue,
Creating hats that hum a tune,
And mittens made for two.

So when you pull your scarf too tight,
Just smile and try to mend,
For every stitch that helps you laugh,
Holds chaos at the end.

Enigmas in the Fabric

Beneath the patterns, truths abound,
Each twist a playful tease,
A polka dot's a riddle, friend,
That tickles like a sneeze.

In plaid, the whispers intertwine,
With stories old and new,
Like how that sock just vanished,
Was it the dog or you?

The stripes hold secrets, black and white,
Of where the mischief went,
And in the folds of every quilt,
A cheeky grin is bent.

So take a peek, don't be afraid,
Unravel every line,
For hidden in the fabric's thoughts,
Are giggles, sweet, and fine.

Memories Sewn with Love

Stitched with laughter, pulled with care,
A patchwork of delight,
Where every color tells a tale,
And sparkles in the light.

Grandma's needle winked and smiled,
At every tiny flaw,
She turned mistakes to merry laughs,
And wrapped us in her shaw.

Each square a dance of yesteryears,
With yarns from every fun,
From birthday hats to silly socks,
Our lives had just begun.

So when you look upon that quilt,
And see a funny face,
Remember love is stitched in time,
With every warm embrace.

The Weft of Whispered Secrets

In threads of gold, the whispers weave,
Of every giggle shared,
They linger on the fabric's edge,
In mischief, lightly bared.

A tapestry of heart and jest,
With patterns all aglow,
Each strand a wink, a knowing smile,
Of things we'll never show.

With every warp and weft that flies,
The stories spin around,
From socks that dance on rainy days,
To shoes that make a sound.

So gather close, let laughter flow,
In every woven thread,
For secrets whispered in the night,
Are tales we never shed.

Threads of Memory

In a box of old shoes, I found a sock,
That danced with my cat, oh what a shock!
It twirled and it spun, a sight to see,
I laughed so hard, it tickled me.

Forgotten receipts tell tales of yore,
Like that time I bought fifty cans—what for?
My fridge was a maze, a canned food bazaar,
But I found a pizza, yes, that's the star.

Grandma's old stories still echo around,
Like the time that her purse went—splat on the ground!
She lost all her coins, they scattered like dust,
We laughed till we cried, oh, in fun we trust.

Under the bed, dust bunnies reside,
They plot with my shoes, they team up with pride.
Their laughter rings out, oh, what a mess,
In the world of funny, they claim to profess.

Whispers of Connection

Every phone call starts with a sneeze,
I blame the cats, they do as they please.
But the laughter that follows makes all the fuss,
Funny how pets can cause such a ruckus.

My buddy sent memes that made me cackle,
A cat in a hat with a sassy little tackle.
We shared our snacks over video calls,
Funny how friendship breaks down the walls.

Old photographs lead to giggles and sighs,
Like the time I wore those oversized ties.
We reminisce about style choices made,
With laughter in gaps, the best plans laid.

Together we stumble through memory's gate,
Past tales of mix-ups that make us relate.
In the humor we find, we're bound ever tight,
Chasing these whispers brings pure delight.

Woven Stories

My dog made a mess with a ball of some yarn,
Now I have a sweater—looks more like a barn!
I wear it with pride, it's a hoot and a half,
Every time I trip, I can't help but laugh.

A tale of lost socks—oh, where do they go?
They vanish like magic, just putting on a show.
I now wear mismatched, a fashionable sin,
Who knew that chaos could feel like a win?

Granddad's wild tales of his youth gone awry,
Like the time he tried to bake, oh my, oh my!
The cake was a flop, but the story was gold,
In the laughter of family, all secrets unfold.

Through moments like these, our lives intertwine,
Each funny mishap a reason to dine.
With giggles and snorts, we build up our lore,
Woven together, who could ask for more?

Bonds That Bind

Two cats on a leash? Oh, what a sight!
They pulled and they tugged—such a funny fight.
With leashes like ropes, they tangled and cried,
In the circus of pets, no one could hide.

Baked a pie once, it rolled off the table,
Chased it down the hall—was I ever able?
The laughter that echoed as it swooshed by fast,
Who knew that my pie would be such a blast?

Neighbors came near, to join in the fun,
With stories and jokes, from everyone.
In the warmth of the crowd, we found our groove,
Laughter and love make our spirits move.

Through quirky adventures, we bond, we confide,
In every mishap, we help one another glide.
With each little moment, we craft, we entwine,
In this funny old dance, our hearts redefine.

Stories Entangled in Time

In a world where clowns do dance,
And time skips like a jolly prance,
Each wiggle tells a tale so neat,
As socks do twirl on tiny feet.

The cat in boots sings opera loud,
While ants parade, a tiny crowd,
A clock with legs, it stops to play,
And munches cookies all the day.

A fish that wears a flashy tie,
Swims through a pond, oh me, oh my!
With leapfrog frogs who flip and flop,
While goofy ducks just cannot stop.

In this odd land of juggled dreams,
Where nothing quite is what it seems,
The stories twist, they twirl and fly,
As laughter paints the azure sky.

Links of a Silent Symphony

There is a snail who plays the flute,
And serenades a dancing root,
While mushrooms jiggle to the beat,
And squirrels provide the rhythm neat.

A hedgehog strums a tiny lute,
With melodies that make you hoot,
The garden blooms with giggles bright,
As daisies join the wild delight.

In this bonkers, jazzy space,
With notes that tickle every face,
The ants in tuxes take the stage,
As laughter turns a solemn page.

So listen close to nature's song,
Where everything feels right, not wrong,
For in this link of whimsy grand,
A silent symphony is planned.

The Weft and Warp of Existence

A tutu-wearing llama prances bright,
While thoughts of knitting loom in flight,
As yarn spins tales on spinning wheels,
The laughter echoes, joyous reels.

A spider knits a quilt of dreams,
With patches sewn of frothy creams,
As crickets chirp in harmony,
Their songs, like whispers, float so free.

A squirrel with glasses reads a book,
With wisdom rare, just take a look,
He shares the tales of skies and trees,
While munching on some extra cheese.

In this fabric of the silly and bold,
Where stories shimmer like spun gold,
The weft and warp entwine with glee,
Creating laughter, wild and free.

Chronicles Embedded in Fabric

A fabric square tells tales of old,
Of wacky pirates, brave and bold,
Who sailed on ships made out of cheese,
And fought with spoons 'gainst mighty fleas.

An apron hosts a chef of dreams,
Whose cakes are large, or so it seems,
With icing that can make you sing,
And cupcakes shaped like roosting things.

A patchwork quilt that warms the night,
Holds stories bathed in laughter's light,
As doodles dance across the seams,
Bringing forth the wackiest dreams.

So gather 'round this fabric lore,
Where silliness is at the core,
For in these threads of humor spun,
Chronicles of joy have just begun.

Narratives of Unity

In a crowd of quirks, we stand side by side,
Sharing laughter and snacks with glee, our guide.
From mishaps to pranks, our adventures unfold,
Every story we tell is worth more than gold.

With our mismatched socks and wild hairdos,
We dance through the chaos, sharing our views.
There's a hilarious mix in our unique blend,
Our giggles unite us, each laugh is a friend.

Woven Threads of Memory

In a fabric of fun, our tales intertwine,
Reminiscing the times when we all felt divine.
With each trip and fall, there's a story to share,
Like the time I tripped over that rogue garden chair.

With snacks in hand and jokes on the plate,
We recount all the moments that make life great.
From old pranks to blunders, our stories reappear,
Every giggle tells secrets that only we hear.

The Silken Bonds Between Us

In a festival of smiles, we gather and beam,
Creating crazy moments, we plot and we scheme.
From wobbly chairs to cake on the floor,
Every misstep we make just opens up more.

With laughter as glue, we stick like some goo,
Reminding each other of what we can do.
Like silly little penguins, we waddle around,
In the love that we share, true joy can be found.

Fragments of Our Shared History

With each crazy mishap, a new gem appears,
Collecting our chuckles, as we down a few beers.
From the dance-offs at noon to the pie-eating spree,
Each fragment of fun builds our sweet history.

Like breadcrumbs trailing through memory lanes,
We giggle at mishaps, and shrug off the pains.
Our laughter's a treasure that binds us with glee,
In the tapestry woven, you're cherished by me.

The Art of Connection

In a world of quirks and funny faces,
We share our secrets in odd places.
A sneeze here, a laugh there too,
Connecting dots like a smudged greeting card blue.

With mismatched socks and a laugh that's loud,
We stumble through life, part of a crowd.
Juggling jokes and our wild spins,
Our stories collide where the chaos begins.

We speak in riddles, toss in a pun,
With every odd glance, another thread spun.
Like wearing a hat that's slightly askew,
We weave a tapestry that's just for our crew.

So raise a toast to the bonds we mishap,
Each giggle and grin is a little love map.
In this dance of the goofy, we find our place,
Connecting the dots in life's hilarious race.

Heartstrings Intertwined

Two left feet on a summer's day,
We trip over words and dance the wrong way.
With laughter bubbling, it's hard to sway,
As heartstrings twist in a playful ballet.

Like spaghetti noodles flung on the wall,
Our stories stick, we laugh till we fall.
In a game of charades where no one can win,
These traps of connection become little spins.

A wink and a nudge, we're silly and bright,
Joking about breakfast at one in the night.
We tickle each other with tales of delight,
Creating a bond that feels just right.

So here's to the humor that draws us so close,
In our quirky gallery, we're the proud hosts.
Each giggle a reminder, each twist a delight,
Together we dance on this whimsical flight.

Threads of Connection

Like cats in a yarn shop, we swipe and we play,
Crafting our stories in the silliest way.
With mismatched colors that twirl and entwine,
These threads of connection, so wacky and fine.

An umbrella that's bent and a laugh that's loud,
We stand side by side in our quirky crowd.
Launching wild puns like a game of old darts,
These simple connections are plump works of art.

We share all our blunders and giggle on cue,
Our mishaps the glue that sticks us like glue.
Like socks that don't match, or a bowl of wet rice,
Each twist in our tales adds flavor and spice.

So toast to the laughter that fills up the air,
Each tumble and trip shows just how we care.
In this fabric of life, we're sewn oh so tight,
Creating a quilt that's both awkward and bright.

Whispers of the Woven

In the chat of the kitchen, our stories unfold,
With whispers and chuckles like secrets retold.
A pinch of salt while we swap our best schemes,
Our laughter's the thread that stitches our dreams.

Each quirky mishap, a banner we wave,
In the fabric of friendship, we're happy and brave.
Like socks with no pair, mismatched but right,
We weave in the humor from morning to night.

With giggles and twirls, we dance through the mess,
Creating a quilt with the moments we bless.
Each wink and a grin is a stitch of delight,
The whispers we share make everything bright.

So gather around for a laugh or two,
These threads we have woven are vibrant and true.
With each twist and turn in our quirky little life,
We savor the whispers that banish all strife.

The Threads that Bind

In a room full of smiles and cheer,
A yarn gets spun, oh-so-dear.
Misplaced socks and tangled hair,
Laughter erupts, without a care.

Popcorn flies when stories ignite,
A cat on the table, what a sight!
We trip on a tale, then stumble and sway,
Chasing our laughter, all night and day.

Unfolding Chronicles

The book is thick, but tales are light,
Each page flips, it's pure delight.
Grandma's tales turn cats into kings,
While Dad's laughs make the whole house sing.

In kitchens, spaghetti meets history,
Sauces fly, a messy mystery.
A dog steals a slice, think he's so sly,
While we chuckle and watch him deny.

Bonds Beyond Measure

A pizza night where toppings collide,
Pineapple chaos, unplanned, side by side.
Chocolate puddles on the floor,
It's messy, it's fun, who could ask for more?

Old friends gather, stories erupt,
With every bite, giggles interrupt.
When the dough rises, so do our dreams,
In the mess, we find the sweetest schemes.

Twists of Shared Destiny

In a world where jokes unwind,
The punchlines dance, oh how they grind.
A kid on a trike rides into the fray,
With dreams of a race, come what may.

A squirrel steals lunch right from our hands,
While we plot and scheme like secret bands.
With every mishap, we find our way,
In this wacky world, we laugh and play.

Interlaced Journeys

We set off on a journey, oh what a sight,
With socks that don't match and shoes too tight.
Our map upside down, a giggle-filled chase,
Lost in our laughter, we pick up the pace.

The phone's battery dead, but we don't really care,
With stories we tell, they float in the air.
My brother gets lost in a tree full of bees,
We're rolling in chaos, yet feel so at ease.

Each stop a new spectacle, snacks on the way,
A sandwich we share, then it flies far away.
The dog snags the crumbs, as we double our glee,
Our journey's a circus, come swing on with me.

At last, we find treasure, it sparkles and glows,
A mystery item, with nobody knows.
"What is it?" we ponder, with squints and with grins,
Our hearts in a twist, we're all winners, not sins.

Snapshots of Kinship

In the family albums, what chaos we find,
Photos of moments, a wild, funny kind.
Uncles in tuxedos, a cat in a hat,
A sprinkle of mayhem, now how about that?

With faces all twisted, and eyes wide like saucers,
We danced in the rain, like a bunch of great authors.
The dog stole the cake, as we roared with delight,
These snapshots of joy always make us feel bright.

A family reunion, we giggle and snack,
The food's a little funny, our hearts share the whack.
A member goes missing, oh where can they be?
Then pops out from nowhere, "Seems I'm stuck in a tree!"

So raise up our glasses, let laughter collide,
With snapshots that capture each joy and wild ride.
We gather, we bumble, our quirks so sublime,
In this circle of love, we are all in our prime.

Embracing the Threads

We weave through our stories, with yarns so bizarre,
Like grandma who knits with a sock on her car.
The patterns we form, with giggles that spread,
Stitches of banter, like sunshine wethread.

A shoelace mishap, a trip, then a laugh,
And auntie's wild hairdo gives half of us gaff.
The colors collide, a vibrant delight,
Creating a tapestry, colorful and bright.

Together we patchwork, a quilt of our days,
With symbols of joy in the most twisted ways.
The family connects in a jangle and mix,
As we sip on our drinks, our world's full of tricks.

In laughter's warm hug, all the fibers align,
Each snip, each embrace, age-old tales intertwine.
So share in our fabric, let's twist and let's spin,
In this funny connection, we all join in!

Connections in Shadows

In the park full of shadows, we spin tales anew,
Of monsters and heroes, just shadows to view.
We slip and we tumble, yet laughter's our guide,
Letting loose our whispers, with friends side by side.

The sun's almost setting, we're lost in our dreams,
Ideas floating high, like sweet, fluffy creams.
A grand twist of fate, as our stories unwind,
Connections like shadows, both silly and blind.

A mishap with ice cream, it lands on my nose,
Making Poppins' escape, everyone knows.
With hugs full of quirk, we go deeper than steep,
In shadows of chuckles, the memories we keep.

So gather 'round quick, let's stitch up the night,
With humor our thread, everything feels right.
Through echoes of laughter, our spirits will shine,
Connections in shadows, forever entwined.

The Unseen Connections

In a room where socks often go,
Two lefts ponder on their woe.
When laundry spins, they lose their mate,
Dancing solo on their fate.

The cat strolls in, claims the stash,
With purrs and leaps, oh what a clash!
She takes a sock, as if it's gold,
While mismatched pairs grow old and bold.

The fridge hums low, knows all the tales,
Of spoons that stir but never sail.
In corners dark, behind the yeast,
Whispers of hide-and-seek, at least.

Each toast pops up, a golden tease,
With butter spreads and jelly breeze.
A spread of laughter fills the air,
In this odd dance, all have a share.

Echoes of an Intricate Weave

A spider spins with sticky strands,
Catching things from wayward hands.
Neighbors peek, with curiosity bait,
'What on earth is there to celebrate?'

A party planned for ants and bugs,
With tiny chairs and cozy rugs.
They chatter loud, a crude banter,
Over crumbs they find, a tiny canter.

The bees join in with a humming cheer,
Wings ablaze, spreading good beer.
The ladybug brings tales of old,
While tiny fish wear crowns of gold.

Together they laugh, lean back in pride,
From sticky woes, they do not hide.
An intricate mess, their lives rearranged,
In this wild tale, nothing's estranged.

Weavings of the Heart

In a cozy nook, hearts gather round,
Knitting stories, a soft sound.
One stitch slips, another shimmies,
As laughter bursts with silly whimsies.

A cat jumps up on a yarn ball spree,
Chasing threads, oh what a sight to see!
While grandpa knits a scarf too long,
A tangled mess becomes a song.

The loom of fate spins funny dreams,
With mismatched colors bursting at the seams.
"Is that a scarf or a blanket for a mouse?"
Laughter echoes through the house.

Tangled yarns, each tale a thread,
Stories woven, never dead.
With needles clicking, tales unfurl,
In this whimsical, patchwork world.

The Unbroken Spectrum

In a garden bright, colors laugh,
While flowers bloom, share their half.
The daisies dance with the bold marigold,
Paint the sun with stories told.

A rainbow slips through the fence,
With jokes so funny, quite intense.
Orange giggles at the shade of blue,
While the purple grins at the nick of dew.

The bees buzz tunes of happy chaos,
Spinning tales around the loss.
"I'm not red, I'm merely orange!"
Chimes the color, quite the floral range.

As petals sway, connections grow,
In hues of laughter, bright and slow.
An unbroken prism, wide and bold,
Through humorous tales, life unfolds.

The Stitched Moments

In the quilt of life, patches abound,
Some are zigzag, others just round.
A thread goes wild, what a sight,
Stitching tales deep into the night.

Grandma's yarn, mixed colors and cheer,
Knitted love, just enough to endear.
With every pull, laughter ensues,
A tapestry woven with funny hues.

Each loop a chuckle, every seam a grin,
A few funny stories waiting to spin.
In tangled knots, the fun finds its way,
To remind us all, life's meant to play!

So let's stitch this moment, quirky and bright,
With threads of hilarity, we'll take flight.
In each snip and snarl, find joy that we crave,
In the fabric of laughter, we're forever brave.

Knotted Memories

Remember the time we tripped on the line,
Caught in a knot, you laughed, 'This is fine!'
With every giggle, our friendship grew,
In those tangled moments, I treasured you.

A bow on your hair, all floppy and free,
You said, 'It's fashion!' Oh, can't you see?
But the wind blew strong, it flew away fast,
Leaving behind memories that forever last.

Like shoes tied together, we stumble with glee,
Wrapped up in chuckles, just you and me.
Each knot like a punchline brings joy to our day,
In this comedy act, we dance and we sway.

So here's to the moments, all woven with care,
Like a messy braid, but we're a cute pair.
In knots of delight, let's laugh till we fall,
These memories we cherish, we savor them all.

Chronicles in Threads

In threads of laughter, tales unfold,
Every goofy glitch, every memory told.
While sewing our stories, stitches go wild,
A patchwork of giggles, so blissfully compiled.

Once I lost buttons, you sewed them on tight,
Awkward but funny, oh what a sight!
Each thread a pathway, to whimsy we roam,
In a fabric of folly, we've made our home.

With colorful yarns, we weave through the years,
Spinning round stories that banish our fears.
In every mishap, there's sunshine to find,
As we gather the threads, two hearts intertwined.

Oh, the chronicles written in colors so bright,
Bring laughter and warmth, like stars in the night.
So let's share our stories, ridiculous and bold,
In this fabric of life, laughter's pure gold.

Paths Woven Together

On a path of missteps, we tumble with style,
With laughter and quirks, we go the extra mile.
Each twist a reminder, a giggle, a tease,
Life's funny journey, full of surprises to seize.

Side by side stumbling, we're stuck in the fray,
But together we shine, come what may.
With socks that don't match and hair askew,
We're the fabric of laughter, just us two.

Every detour we take, every silly spree,
Paints brushstrokes of joy, just you and me.
Paths tangled in humor, beautifully bent,
In this dance of mishaps, our hearts are content.

So here's to the journeys, spun with pure glee,
As we weave our adventures, just you and me.
Woven in laughter, let's forever roam,
In the paths we create, we've crafted our home.

Stitched Narratives

In a cozy nook, a cat sat,
With yarn and a ball, he wore a hat.
His thoughts ran wild, like a kite in the sky,
As he plotted to catch that pesky fly.

A sock went missing, much to our grief,
The plot thickens, like a comic relief.
Was it the dog? Or the sneaky gerbil?
Both suspects dance, twirling in a whirl.

When life throws stitches, we laugh and sigh,
For in every knot, there's a reason why.
A tale of mismatched shoes on a spree,
What fun it is to be silly and free!

And when grandma knits with a wink and a grin,
She tells us tales where the fun begins.
With every purl and delightful spin,
The laughter grows, as the stories begin.

Stories Entwined in Shadows

In a shadowy corner, a tale we weave,
Of a ghost who forgot how to leave.
He tripped on a rug, then fell with a scream,
A blunder so silly, it felt like a dream.

With whispers of fabric, the cobwebs play,
As they dance with glee at the end of the day.
Every story we tell from corners so dark,
Sprinkles of laughter in the park.

A moonlight meeting of mischief and cheer,
As shadows giggle, drawing ever near.
The pumpkin carriage rolls, but wait! What's this?
A worm in a tux—oh, how could we miss?

With tales that twist and shadows that laugh,
Our hearts grow lighter, like a dance on a raft.
So join the fun in the dimmest glow,
For every shadow has stories to show!

The Loom of Our Existence

On the loom of life, each thread is a jest,
A woven mishap, a riddle at best.
With colors so bright, yet tangled and wild,
We laugh at the fabric, each adult-like child.

A button goes missing, alone on the floor,
It rolls to a story, as we all implore.
"Where did you go?" we all chirp and plead,
"I'm here for the party—a festive deed!"

We stitch our tales with laughter, you see,
Each knot binding us, oh so merrily.
From tangled up yarn, new friendships arise,
In the fabric of life, we find our surprise.

So gather your threads, let's create and scheme,
For weaving together ignites every dream.
In the loom of our days, so funny, so free,
A tapestry bright, in sweet harmony!

Intertwinings of Life

In life's crazy quilt, we patch and we prod,
With mischief afoot, we giggle and nod.
Two socks on the run, just out of the wash,
They plan their escape with a very loud posh.

A whispering breeze tells secrets at night,
Of mishaps and giggles, all under moonlight.
An ant in a hat, a ladybug's dance,
Who knew they would be the stars of romance?

We interlace stories with laughter so sweet,
Like sandwiches cut with their crusts offbeat.
Each slice of our lives, an odd little feast,
Where even the quiet hold tales at least.

So bring all your tales, let them twirl and spin,
For life's greatest joys, well, they start from within.
In the tapestry woven of strange and of fun,
We find that together, all's said and all's done!

Echoes of Heritage

In grandma's tales, a pickle's dance,
A cat in socks, not left to chance.
Great-uncle Fred, with mutton chops,
Danced with cheese, until he flops.

Cousins gathered, fierce debate,
Which ice cream flavor seals their fate?
The sprinkles flew, a sugar storm,
As laughter swells, they take their form.

Old photos whisper, secrets shared,
A mustache here, a laugh we dared.
From family lore to silly cheer,
Echoes of joy, forever near.

So raise a glass to those we miss,
A toast to laughter, pure bliss!
In every yarn, a thread so bright,
Heritage wrapped in humor's light.

Fabric of Fate

A sock mismatched, a story spun,
In laundry wars, no one has won.
A yarn that's tangled, full of jest,
It wraps around, a game of guess.

The grandma's quilt, a patchwork tale,
With patterns bold, like a wild gale.
Each square a moment, laughter sewn,
In colors bright, our joy displayed.

The dog on skateboards, what a sight,
Chasing the cat, oh what a fright!
A tethered kite flies up so high,
Life's fabric weaves, beneath the sky.

So let's embrace this vibrant thread,
With fists of fun, our worries shed.
In every stitch, a chuckle waits,
In destiny's weave, we celebrate.

Links of Laughter

Two spoons clink in morning light,
A cereal duel, a frothy fight.
Breakfast antics, toast on head,
Sing songs of joy, just like they said.

A chain of jokes, each punchline glows,
Connecting hearts, as laughter flows.
With every giggle, bonds grow tight,
A wobbly dance can feel just right.

Ticklish ribs and silly faces,
In every room, love interlaces.
Grandpa's stories, a great delight,
Woven in laughter, day to night.

So gather 'round, the links we find,
In laughter's net, we're intertwined.
From goofy moments, make it last,
In joy's embrace, our futures cast.

Chronicles Unraveled

In dusty books, forgotten schemes,
A tale of goats and their wild dreams.
With capes of plaid, they chased the sun,
Adventures brewed, oh what fun!

Each family saga, twists and turns,
In crazy antics, the passion burns.
A chicken's choir, they take the stage,
With feathery flair, they steal the page.

An uncle's secret, an artful prank,
A pie in the face, oh how we prank!
From chaotic spills to belly laughs,
Chronicles weave their playful paths.

So grab a seat, let stories flow,
In each wild chapter, let laughter grow.
With every word, old bonds revive,
In the heart of tales, we come alive.

Patterns of Togetherness

In a world where socks go missing,
We find them in the strangest places.
A dance of oddities is glistening,
As we laugh at misplaced laces.

Who knew that keys have minds of their own?
They hide till we search and shout with glee.
Like socks with their mates, as we've grown,
We'll bond over lost items, you and me.

The chair with three legs has stories to share,
Each wobble a giggle from times long past.
Life's quirks are the patterns we wear,
Laughing together, a bond that will last.

So here's to the moments, absurd and bright,
Where laughter weaves us, both near and far.
In the fabric of life, joy takes flight,
As we create our unique memoir.

Threads of the Past

A tangled mess of holiday lights,
Reminds us of grandma's festive cheer.
As she swears she remembers the rights,
To find the end — a zany frontier!

Old sweaters hold stories, like stains of the years,
When we dined with hot sauce and spilled our drink.
Each thread a chuckle, with joyful tears,
In the warmth of nostalgia, we all find our link.

The photos with faces that seem to frown,
Caught mid-blink, a moment in attire.
We laugh at ourselves, no need for a crown,
In the ride through the past, we never tire.

Each memory's like a yarn ball untold,
Round and round it goes, spinning with laughter.
The crazy weaves a tale to behold,
As we bond over chaos — happily after!

Stories Woven by Stars

Under the moonlight, we gather and scheme,
The stories we tell take flight on a breeze.
Of aliens abducting our ice cream,
And midnight escapades, aiming to please.

Stargazing, we plot with a pizza surprise,
Silly conspiracies laced with delight.
Each shooting star, just a wink to our eyes,
Like quirky wishes spun on a night bright.

And when we bump heads, scaring the night,
It's laughter that stitches our fumbled parade.
Creating constellations of pure delight,
With every strange wish that we've ever made.

Together, we write an astral charade,
Mischief and warmth in the cosmos above.
With every bright tale and silly escapade,
We twinkle together, the essence of love.

Unity in the Strands

As we weave through the quirks of each day,
Life's shoelaces tangle, but who really cares?
With laughter, we trip but still find a way,
To smile at our fumbles, in fun-filled affairs.

The puzzle of friends, each piece a delight,
Some edge pieces, others, just round.
With giggles and grins, we all unite,
Creating a picture where joy can be found.

The jelly spills purple, a mess on the floor,
We dance around it, our hearts filled with cheer.
Every blunder a banquet we can't ignore,
With unity found, and nothing to fear.

In the strands of our lives, humor shines through,
We're a tapestry woven of laughter so bright.
Through every adventure and silly hullabaloo,
Together we thread a most memorable night.

The Knots We Share

In a room full of shoes, things get quite wild,
My left foot's in trouble, the right one's a child.
They argue all day, in a dance quite absurd,
While I chase after socks, oh, how they just blurred.

A cat with a yarn ball, what madness unfolds,
Tangled up giggles, the story it told.
Each string that it chews, leads to new mishaps,
In a world made of laughter, with whimsical snaps.

Grandma's old stories, they're juicy and bright,
Like knitting up dreams, in the soft evening light.
Each poke is a punchline, each stitch brings a grin,
When we gather together, the laughter begins.

Oh, the puzzles we weave, an odd tapestry,
With each thread combined, pure comedy.
We laugh 'til we cry, weaving jokes without end,
In the knots that we share, love's a grand blend.

Stories Stitched in Time

In a quilt made of whispers, secrets unfold,
Grandpa lost his marbles, or so I've been told.
He stitched in a chuckle, a patch made of cheer,
With buttons for eyes, it's as funny as beer.

A time traveler's yarn, spun with giggly glee,
With loops and with twists, he fell in a tree.
Each tale has a tickle, a twist to the plot,
From crumpets to comets, oh, the laughter's a lot.

At dinner, we argue about who has the best,
With forks as our swords, we'll put jokes to the test.
The punchlines, they fly like mashed potatoes foul,
In this funny old kitchen, we laugh and we howl.

Those stories we weave, a ridiculous spree,
Like knitting with spaghetti, oh, can't you see?
With threads of our lives, we stitch jokes entwined,
In funny old patterns, our laughter aligned.

Interlaced Journeys

A traveler stumbles, caught in a bind,
With shoelaces tangled, oh, isn't it kind?
He trips on his tales, a bumbling delight,
Each story he tells simply adds to the plight.

At the fair, I spun round, lost my hat in the breeze,
A clown grabbed my collar, brought me down to my knees.
Laughing with strangers, whose socks don't quite match,
Finding humor in chaos—what a beautiful patch!

In a bus full of folks, we shared silly jokes,
With laughter contagious, we became the best folks.
Each mile added memories, stitches of fun,
In a patchwork of stories, we all came undone.

Road trips are perfect for weaving these threads,
Where antics and laughter end up in our heads.
From detours to mishaps, what a joyful scene,
Interlaced journeys, with laughter between.

Chronicles of Connection

In a web made of stories, where giggles abound,
Each squabble a fable, a laugh gets around.
With spoons as our swords, we joust for the pies,
The chronicles written with crumbs in our eyes.

A dog steals a sausage, a chase in full swing,
Barking out punches and clapping in spring.
Each wag of the tail, a tale in disguise,
With laughter resounding, oh, what a surprise!

Around the campfire, tales flicker with flair,
Funny old shadows dance high in the air.
With marshmallows toasted, we share all our glee,
Creating connections that only we see.

In the stories we share, old friendships ignite,
With laughter as glue, making everything right.
As we gather together, in silliness shine,
Chronicles of connection, uniquely divine.

Frayed Edges of History

In a crooked old house, a cat wore a hat,
Chasing shadows where memories sat.
The stories they tell, with a wink and a grin,
Like socks in the dryer, they twist and they spin.

Grandma's old sweater, with patches so bright,
Tells tales of her youth, a funny old sight.
In a quilted embrace of odd little dreams,
Laughter erupts as her humor redeems.

A maiden once tripped on her own flowing veil,
And a prince laughed so hard, he forgot to exhale.
With mishaps and giggles, love found its way,
In the frayed edges, bright hues took the stage.

Like a jigsaw undone, pieces flying high,
Each knot in the fabric brings forth a sly sigh.
In the tapestry's quirks, we learn and we play,
Life spills out stories in the funniest way.

Tapestries of Unseen Bonds

In the attic's gloom, a dusty old trunk,
Holds socks that eloped, by mischief they're sunk.
Each fabric's a secret, a giggle, a clue,
We wear mismatched stories, just me and you.

A dog with a leash that's tangled with shoes,
Is plotting a course of whimsical news.
He barks to the stars, making sense of the night,
While dreams dance around him, in joyful delight.

The hats that we sport tell the tales that we weave,
Of moments that trick us, we tumble, believe.
Each verrrry loose button might loosen a laugh,
As we share our blunders at love's happy graph.

Uncommon connections are threads in the light,
We gather them close, like a hug oh-so-tight.
In the fabric of life, stitched with great care,
The unseen bonds shimmer, twinkling in air.

The Hidden Threads of Belonging

A sandwich once spoke, with a crusty old joke,
"Why did the pickle refuse to provoke?"
It sat on the plate, with a smirk just so sly,
In a picnic of giggles beneath the blue sky.

Old photos reveal, many awkward affairs,
Like dances with llamas and wearing mismatched pairs.
Each snapshot a giggle, a wink of the past,
In the history of blunders, hilarity's cast.

A teddy bear grins, with a fluff-tail of yarn,
Claiming to have had adventures so far'n.
He points to a tale of a mischievous sprite,
Who painted the night with his giggles and fright.

In a circle of friends, we tell tales so grand,
Of moments that bind, like a slapstick band.
With each hidden thread, we find joy in the mess,
For belonging is laughter, in all its finesse.

Lyrical Interlaces

In a garden of puns, flowers bloom with a twist,
Each petal a punchline, impossible to resist.
The bees buzz along, with a wink and a dance,
As humor unravels, in a whimsical trance.

There's a broomstick that's dancin', two mops that sing,
Creating a symphony, oh what joy they bring!
With laughter that rises from the roots of the ground,
Each note in the air, like a quirky rebound.

A mischievous cat with a flair for the funny,
Steals socks from the line, thinking, "Aren't I so sunny?"
Each chase is a story, a parade of delight,
In the fabric of joy that we share through the night.

In the world of the zany, connections we find,
Interlaced with chuckles, uniquely designed.
With lyrical threads that twine through our hearts,
We dance in the laughter, that life's humor imparts.

Threads of Shared Experience

In the closet hangs a coat,
A relic of a long-lost vote.
We wore it once to dance in light,
Now it stirs up laughter, bright.

A tale of socks that went astray,
A pair once loved, now lost in play.
Did they escape to join a band?
Or purposely take that sock's grand stand?

The cat once wore that silly hat,
Who knew she'd strut like a diplomat?
We snapped a pic, now it's a meme,
Our furry friend, the social theme!

So let us weave these moments tight,
With quirky jokes that feel just right.
Our threads of laughter never fray,
In silly dreams, we dance and sway.

Whispers of the Untold

A banana peel, a well-timed slip,
With giggles shared, we lost our grip.
The neighbors peered from window frames,
While we played stealthy, sneaky games.

A secret shake, a silly face,
Tales of cats that dream of space.
From lost goldfish to a dancing broom,
These funny whispers start to bloom.

We wrote our stories on the wall,
With sticky notes and a grand recall.
"Oh, remember when?" they'd always say,
Laughter lingered through the day.

In shared absurdity, we find our zest,
With every quirk, we're truly blessed.
The joy of silly bonds we mold,
Are treasures kept, untold, and bold.

Journeys Bound by Words

Two friends set sail on a cluttered boat,
With maps made out of pizza dough.
They searched for treasure—peace of mind,
But found a stash of jelly beans, oh so fine!

The compass spun in circles wild,
As laughter rang, a carefree child.
With each tall tale that filled the air,
They wove a journey, beyond compare.

In the park, their shadows danced,
Over tacos, they took a chance.
Inventing worlds with just a word,
Where nothing's quite as it's occurred.

With quips exchanged, and funny truths,
Wanderers in a land of youths.
These journeys mixed—both spicy and sweet,
With every laugh, they found their beat.

The Spectrum of Connection

A joke about a pickle's plight,
Has colors bright as neon light.
It wraps around our hearts so free,
Uniting all like a family tree.

From puns that pop like bubble gum,
To tales of moose that dance with drums.
Each laugh a shade, a bright facade,
In every smile, a joyful nod.

We mix our moments in a bowl,
With flavors bold, we reach our goal.
Adding spice like cayenne zest,
A recipe for joy, the very best!

So raise a toast with waffle fries,
Embrace the fun in every guise.
Through colors mixed, our spirits rise,
For moments shared are our great prize.

The Unseen Weave

In a world where chaos roams,
Threads misbehave like cheeky gnomes.
One thread sings, another dances,
They cross paths, taking wild chances.

Patterns form with a twist and twirl,
Knots in the fabric make laughter swirl.
A sock in a sandwich, bizarre but true,
That's what you get when threads are askew.

A button flew off during a spree,
Joined a riddle with a cup of tea.
The grandma stitched with a smirk on her face,
Said, "Every stitch finds its rightful place!"

So here's to the weavers, the jesters of thread,
Crafting a story that's silly instead.
With spools of laughter and fabric of cheer,
In the realm of the stitch, there's no room for fear.

Tales in Every Stitch

A needle poked a weary yarn,
"Let's make a quilt, not a barn!"
With colors bright and patterns grand,
Each stitch whispers of a comical land.

A plaid and polka dot bicker at night,
Who wore the silliest, who wears it right?
A bobbin rolls in a dizzy spree,
"I'm the real star, just wait and see!"

A patchwork goat joins the playful fray,
Its laughter stitches the blues away.
A tale told over snacks and jam,
"Every patch has a past, just like grandma!"

So let's gather 'round with thread and cheer,
For every stitch brings a tale near.
In this fabric world of antics and zest,
Let's weave funny tales, we're truly blessed!

Silent Threads

In the silence, threads have fun,
Ticklish whispers, no need to run.
A thread by itself can cause a stir,
Bouncing around like a curious blur.

In corners, they giggle, in shadows, they play,
Making mischief while we're away.
A single strand tries to break free,
But gets tangled in a cup of tea!

A button looks on with an eye so sly,
"Let's launch a threadcraft, oh my, oh my!"
They conspire to create a grand prank,
A silly sock puppet in the kitchen plank.

So if you hear giggles from fabric tight,
It's threads having fun on a whimsical night.
In stitches and seams, the laughter spreads,
In the silence, it's dreams that they thread.

Tapestry of Time

In a tapestry where seconds reside,
Threads play hopscotch, and time takes a ride.
A minute gets lost in a fabric swirl,
While hours do cartwheels, giving a twirl.

Patterns collide in a merry dance,
Each misstep leads to a newfound chance.
A clock that chimes with a jester's grin,
Reminds us to laugh, let the fun begin!

A zipper zipped up from dusk till dawn,
Claimed it could fly, that silly spawn.
Said, "I'll race the stars, just watch me zoom!"
But ended up tangled in a wild costume.

So here's to the threads that charm the hours,
Creating moments with magical powers.
In this fabric realm, let's spin and rhyme,
Forever a part of this tapestry of time.

www.ingramcontent.com/pod-product-compliance
Lightning Source LLC
Chambersburg PA
CBHW070305120526
44590CB00017B/2568